EUCLID

The Great Geometer

EUCLID

The Great Geometer

Chris Hayhurst

The Rosen Publishing Group, Inc., New York

Published in 2006 by The Rosen Publishing Group, Inc.
29 East 21st Street, New York, NY 10010

First Edition

Library of Congress Cataloging-in-Publication Data

Hayhurst, Chris.
Euclid: the great geometer / Chris Hayhurst.—1st ed.
   p. cm.—(The library of Greek philosophers)
Includes bibliographical references.
ISBN 1-4042-0497-0 (lib. bdg.)
1. Euclid. 2. Mathematicians—Greece—Biography.
3. Mathematics, Greek. 4. Geometry.
I. Title. II. Series.
QA29.E78H39 2006
510'.92—dc22
                        2005006692

Manufactured in the United States of America

On the cover: Detail from a fifteenth-century tile showing an artist's representation of Euclid. Background: Detail of Raphael's *School of Athens.*

CONTENTS

INTRODUCTION

Two thousand years ago, the world was a very different place than it is today. There was no Internet, of course. Nor were there computers, televisions, stereos, microwaves, or electronics of any sort. Cars did not exist. Neither did bikes, skateboards, or Rollerblades.

It was a much smaller world then, though not in a literal sense. The planet was the same size it is today, and it traveled the same looping path around the sun that it does now. The world was much smaller in the sense that the people who lived in it knew very little about it. What they did know about was usually only the land on which they lived. Perhaps they had vague notions of other lands far away, much farther than they would ever dream of traveling. Daily life, for most, was the same routine. It was waking in the morning, working by day, and sleeping by night.

For some, however, including those who found themselves tucked into the lush and prosperous lands surrounding the Mediterranean Sea, the world of more than 2,000 years ago was also a time of intense intellectual investigation. People asked questions and wondered about life. They also pondered the meaning of existence and whether it held any significance beyond what they could see before them. They were thinkers and dreamers, inventors and creators. They found an importance to life that those before them had never considered. They began to see the world as a place for unearthing answers to life's mysteries.

Forget, if just for a while, the things that surround you, and instead submerse yourself in a world where life itself is a mystery. Step out of your chair and into the blue and green of the ancient Mediterranean Sea. Wade into the waters, as far as you dare. Set your imagination free. And then, if you can, turn around and look back toward the shore.

Welcome to ancient Greece. It's 300 BC, more than 2,300 years ago. Before you, in a stone-walled courtyard surrounded by olive trees, stands an assortment

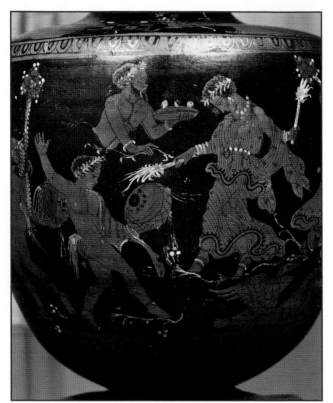

A Dionysian scene of revelry is depicted on this fourth-century-BC Greek vase. Dionysus was the ancient Greek god of wine, and many feasts and parties were held each year in his honor. Considered a benevolent god, Dionysus was also associated with peace, agriculture, and the theater.

of people like you've never seen before. All of them are men. They stand in clusters, talking among themselves in loud, boisterous bursts of laughter. They hold wine in what look like large, heavy earthen mugs. They drink the wine like water and eat ferociously from enormous tables made of thick, dark wood. Many of the men have long, gray beards. All have dense manes of scraggly hair. They stand barefoot or in sandals. Their clothes are light and robelike, just right for the warm winds that blow in from the nearby sea.

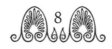

The men's voices grow louder as the sun begins to set. Servants move among the partygoers, replenishing the food as quickly as it is consumed. Finally, as the darkness sets in, one man pulls himself onto a table and stands well above the rest. A flaming torch just a few feet behind him sends his shadow dancing and leaping across the courtyard. The man raises his drink high above his head and, with dark, thoughtful eyes, looks out over his peers. The crowd grows silent. The man toasts someone named Euclid. And with that, the people, who have now all turned to face one man standing alone near the center of the courtyard, raise their drinks in the toast.

But wait. Let's take a step back. Who exactly is this man Euclid, or Euclid of Alexandria, sometimes Euclides of Alexandria, as some have called him? And why is he, of all people, the hero of the evening? What did he do to deserve such a celebration?

Euclid was a mysterious man, almost more a legend than a real-life, flesh-and-blood historical figure. He did live in ancient Greece, that much we know for sure. And he did leave his mark on the world, mainly through one tremendously important book that he wrote. But beyond that, the rest is almost entirely speculation. Historians specializing in ancient Greece have dug through countless artifacts, searching for

EVCLIDI MEGAREN·

This fifteenth-century painting of Euclid shows the great geometer using a compass to make a calculation. Euclid produced a number of significant mathematical works, but his most famous was a book called *The Elements*. *The Elements* contained everything known about geometry at that time, and was required reading for mathematicians for hundreds of years.

clues to the particulars of Euclid's life. Almost nothing has been found.

But some things are known. Euclid, a mathematician, was born during Greece's Classical Age. This was a time, typically considered to be between around 530 BC and 300 BC, of unprecedented scientific, political, and philosophical progress and innovation. Many brilliant people lived during this time, producing works that would change the world. They weren't afraid to ask questions that had never been asked before, and they never hesitated to break new intellectual ground.

In Euclid's case, this new ground was clear: it was the subject of mathematics, specifically geometry. Euclid took geometry to an entirely new level. It was he, perhaps more than anyone before him or after him, who shaped the subject into what it is today. As a result, he become known as the father of geometry.

Before we go deeper into Euclid's life, though, we must first look at the lives and times of those who came before him. Euclid, after all, was a product of his times, the result of the centuries of thought and progress that came before him. It was the great English mathematician and physicist Sir Isaac Newton who gave credit to his own predecessors with the following exclamation: "If I have seen further, it is by standing upon the shoulders of giants." Euclid, had he been alive during Newton's time to read those words, would have almost certainly agreed. Euclid, too, stood on the shoulders of giants. And he, like Newton, saw further than those who preceded him.

ANCIENT GREECE

When we talk about Euclid, who is generally believed to have lived from around 325 to 265 BC, we can't do so without talking about ancient Greece.

"Ancient Greece" is a vague term, referring to a period of time that most historians agree ranges from about 800 to 150 BC, or 2,800 to 2,150 years ago.

Much of what we love and enjoy about society today can be traced all the way back to the ancient Greeks. Take democracy, for instance. Democracy is the foundation of a free society in much of the world today. Without democracy, we wouldn't be allowed to vote for our leaders, stand up for our beliefs, or speak out against those with whom we disagree. Democracy allows people to play an active role in government and the management and day-to-day affairs of their nation. Democracy grants us the freedom to live the way we choose.

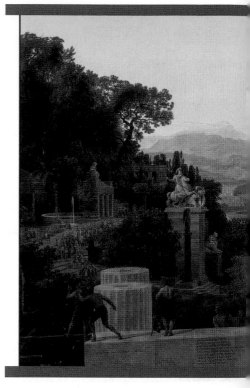

Democracy owes its birth to ancient Greece, especially to the greatest Greek city of that time, Athens. Back then, "democracy" was known by the Greek word *demokratia*, for "rule of the people." It was such an important concept to the Greeks that they even had a goddess, Demokratia, named after it.

This was in the time of the Greek Classical Age, the period of time just before the beginning of the Persian War in 490 BC, and just after the death of Alexander the Great in 323 BC. This time was characterized by not only great battles, but also great literature and tremendous advances in philosophy, art, and science.

ATHENS

Athens, a bustling metropolis ("metropolis" is another Greek word) near the end of a long finger of land

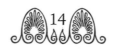

This 1825 oil painting by Karl Friedrich Schinkel shows Greece the way it might have looked during Euclid's time. Ancient Greek culture was extremely advanced, and many aspects of modern Western culture can be traced back to the ancient Greeks. Many advances in mathematics were made during this time as well. Euclid's work laid the foundation for modern geometry.

jutting out toward the Mediterranean Sea, was the cultural center of the Greek-speaking world.

People came to Athens from all around to see the latest art exhibits and to go to the theater. Busy street markets carried fresh fruits and vegetables

and fish—all the food a person would need to feed a family. The city thrived on the very fact that it was a place to gather in public, to meet new and interesting people, and to be a part of the bubbling energy that was Athens.

Not surprisingly, Athens, being a cultural center, also managed to attract the brightest intellectuals of the time. The city's force was almost magnetic. Some of the greatest writers, philosophers, and mathematicians in Greece migrated to Athens. They did so for good reason. The atmosphere of a place like Athens could stimulate the mind, and move great thinkers to develop new ideas. Intellectuals from all over Greece would gather and talk for hours.

These intellectuals, including philosophers (from the Greek word *philosophos*, for those who "love wisdom"), were guaranteed the right to speak their minds because of the democratic society in which they lived. Greek democracy allowed certain people (not all, as we'll see), "citizens," liberty in two specific ways. First, they had the political freedom to take part in the democratic process. They could speak at public meetings, vote for new laws or amendments to existing laws, and generally participate in the workings of government. Second, they had the freedom to do what they wished in their private lives. In other words, when among family and friends, or even just acquaintances, they could speak their minds without fear of persecution.

While this democracy might sound similar to the democracy we live in now, there were some important differences. One difference was that in Athenian democracy, equality was merely guaranteed in politics, not in social or economic life. A poor man who participated in the Athenian democratic process could vote and speak out, but that didn't mean he'd be granted an opportunity to move up in life, or to achieve wealth or improved social status. Today, for example, if you're born to a poor family you can find opportunities to work your way out of poverty. You can go to school with the help of grants and loans from the government. And any career is potentially yours, if you're willing to put in the work to get you there. In ancient Athens, on the other hand, a man on the bottom usually stayed at the bottom.

Another difference—and by far the most important difference—was that not all those who lived in Athens were considered citizens. In order to have political rights, you had to be a citizen. In early Athens, only adult male residents who weren't slaves were guaranteed citizenship. Women, foreigners, children, and

Slavery in Ancient Greece

Slaves were common in ancient Greece, so common, in fact, that some historians believe that, in the cities especially, there may have been more slaves than free people.

Slaves came from all walks of life. Some people became slaves as young children, either born into slavery because their parents were slaves or were sold into slavery by their impoverished family. Other children became slaves after being abandoned as infants by their parents.

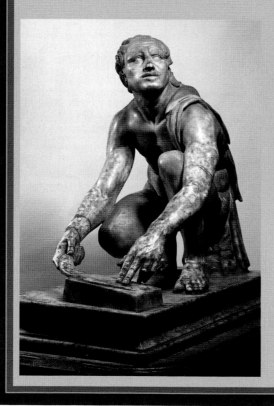

Although Greek culture was very advanced in some ways, the cruel practice of slavery was widespread. Much of ancient Greece's economy was dependent on the practice of slavery. Many slaves were prisoners captured during military campaigns. Although it was not a common practice, slaves could be freed by their owners.

They would be picked up by a stranger and sold to the wealthy. Once taken in by a rich family, they were destined to a life of servitude.

Other people became slaves when they were captured during war. Ancient Greece was a time of much upheaval, and battles raged constantly for many years. When enemy cities were captured, they were looted by the invading army. Any survivors were forced into a life of slavery.

In a city like Athens, slaves were everywhere. The wealthiest of families often relied on up to twenty slaves at a time to help them run their households. Other slaves worked as laborers, doing everything from cleaning streets to building and maintaining ships. Anywhere there was work to be done, slaves were there. Almost every job was a slave's job.

slaves, on the other hand, lacked the political rights of their adult male counterparts.

For those lucky enough to be considered citizens—that is, free men older than the age of eighteen—democracy was an integral part of daily life. Experts today believe there were somewhere around 30,000 adult males living in Athens during Euclid's time who fell into this category. This was in a city about the size of Toledo, Ohio, with an overall population of around 300,000.

As it was, Athenian democracy permitted any citizen to speak out at the so-called Public Assembly. Citizens could also vote at the assemblies, which were typically held several dozen times per year on Athens's Pnyx hill. Meetings took place outside in the open air, not far from the famous Acropolis. Speakers would climb onto a platform called a bema to deliver speeches. These enormous meetings would attract thousands of citizens, many of whom took turns voicing their thoughts about the matters at hand. Everything pertaining to state affairs was discussed, including both domestic and foreign policy initiatives.

After sometimes lengthy discussions and debates, issues were decided by a vote. An individual made his choice known by raising his hand. Hands were counted—or at least estimated—and a final decision was made.

This type of democracy is now known as a direct democracy. Unlike the representative or parliamentary democracies typical of today, the citizens who took part in Athenian democracy directly influenced government. They didn't choose people to represent them at government meetings. They went to those meetings themselves.

Ruins are all that are left of the platform from which political speeches were given on Pnyx hill. The Greeks invented democracy nearly 2,500 years ago, and it became a cornerstone of ancient Greek culture. Still, there are many differences in the sort of democracy practiced in ancient Greece and democracy as it is practiced today.

A WORLD OF WAR

The name Alexander the Great has, for more than 2,000 years, signified one man's focused quest to conquer and rule the world. While Athens practically bubbled over with its new democratic ambitions, the Greek leader Alexander set out to become the greatest conqueror the world had ever known.

In Alexander's world, kings ruled over enormous stretches of land. Armies marched hundreds, even thousands, of miles on foot to conquer remote cities and expand their empires. Soldiers could be forced to march for days over difficult terrain, and many died of exhaustion or malnourishment. But it was all for a cause. At that time, it was common for leaders to try to build the largest empire they could.

This was the logic in the ancient kingdom of Macedon, located in approximately the same region as present-day Macedonia, just north of modern Greece. In 359 BC, Macedon was just one of several kingdoms belonging to ancient Greece, but it was also rapidly becoming the most powerful, and Philip II was its ruler.

THE ROMAN REPUBLIC AT TH DEATH OF CAESAR 44 B.C.

Roman territory
States dependent on Rome
Parthian Empire
All names are given in their Latin form

This map shows the territory of the Roman Empire in 44 BC, the year that Julius Caesar was assassinated. Caesar was a brilliant leader, and he helped transform Rome into one of the most powerful empires the world has ever known. Alexander the Great (*inset*), seen here in this detail from a first-century mosaic, was another great conqueror. Although Alexander died while still in his early thirties, he is regarded as one of history's greatest military leaders.

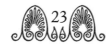

But Philip II's days were numbered, and in 336 BC he was murdered.

It just so happened that Philip II had a son. In ancient Greece, sons of kings succeeded their fathers. Alexander, born in 356 BC (three years into his father's rule), took the throne at the age of twenty. Alexander picked up right where his father had left off, almost immediately embarking on a campaign to conquer the entire known world. Alexander's forces conquered lands from Egypt in North Africa to parts of present-day India and the Persian Gulf.

Philip II of Macedonia's vision of conquest was carried out by his son, Alexander. A brilliant military leader in his own right, Philip paid his army enough money that a man could afford to be a full-time soldier. This greatly expanded the size of Philip's military force.

Thanks to his powerful and relentless army, his holdings grew bigger by the day.

Even the most powerful of rulers eventually die, and for Alexander, death came early. Medicine at the time was not nearly as effective as it is today, and in 323 BC, Alexander the Great succumbed to a fever and died. He was just thirty-two.

As Alexander the Great's empire spread across the world, so, too, did the cultural ideals of Greece. The Classical Age that had once been confined to a relatively small region took hold wherever Alexander, who had been educated in Athens by such great philosophers as Aristotle, and his armies set foot.

Hellenism, as the culture and lifestyle of the time after his death became known, was tremendously popular. Greek civilization, and everything it represented, was growing by the day. All aspects of progressive Greek life gradually took hold of the world's imagination. People saw promise in Hellenism, perhaps as their ticket to a better future.

A STRUGGLE FOR POWER

When Alexander died, there was an immediate grab for power. There were many of the former king's Diadochi, or successors. These men included Alexander's top army generals, the men who had led countless soldiers into battle in the name of expanding their leader's empire. Each of the generals believed he deserved to personally rule at least part of the land that was now without a king. Not surprisingly, things quickly became bloody. The struggle for power was ferocious.

One of those to emerge from the carnage was Alexander's topmost general, Ptolemy I. Ptolemy I headed for Egypt, where he became king of a land whose prize possession was the city of Alexandria, which Alexander the Great had founded in 331 BC, eight years before his death.

Alexandria was in an ideal location—it was right on the Mediterranean, tucked between two branches of the beautiful Nile River. The city had yet to be completed, being fairly new, so Ptolemy's first mission was to finish its construction. He did so quickly, employing huge numbers of people to get the work done. When the city was finished, Ptolemy, perhaps in honor of his fallen leader, declared Alexandria Egypt's new capital.

THE MUSEUM

Ptolemy's vision for the city closely resembled Athens, and he set out to make Alexandria one of

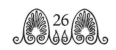

This fourth-century silver coin shows the profile of Ptolemy I, one of Alexander the Great's generals. Ptolemy had extremely good diplomatic and strategic skills, and would go on to rule Egypt after Alexander's death.

the world's top educational centers. Toward that end, the leader of Egypt built what became known as the Museum. Unlike the museums of today, which typically offer numerous artifacts and displays, this huge, luxurious complex was designed for teaching and for research.

Students came to the Museum from all over the world. They studied together, went to class together, ate together, and lived together on the Museum's grounds. Surrounded by lavish courts and beautiful gardens, containing libraries stocked with thousands of scrolls of the world's most respected writings, and complete with an adjacent zoo, the Museum quickly became renowned as the primary institution for higher education. Students, many of whom were among the

most important intellectuals of the time, not only learned the essential subjects of the day, but also taught them. Math, astronomy, science, and medicine were almost everything a man of classical Greece needed to know, and they could all be mastered at the Museum. It was a place for ideas, debate, and progress. It was also the home of a man who many believe was its greatest teacher: Euclid.

2 THE ORIGINS OF MATHEMATICS

There are many ways in which ancient Greek society nurtured innovation and the exploration of new ideas. However, we should focus on the one subject important to Euclid: mathematics.

The word "mathematics" derives from the Greek word meaning "things that have been learned." Mathematics owes much of its progress and development to the intellectuals of ancient Greece's Classical Age. These intellectuals ranged from Thales, who is believed to have invented the subject of geometry (a branch of mathematics that deals with measurements and relationships between points, lines, and shapes), to Pythagoras, who more than anyone else managed to make mathematics a subject for the masses. Finally, Euclid, as we'll see, took mathematics and geometry to an entirely new level.

The Rhind Papyrus is nearly 4,000 years old. Bound in a scroll, the papyrus is thirteen inches (thirty-three centimeters) high and sixteen-and-a-half feet (five meters) long. Before the invention of paper, people wrote on papyrus, which was first invented in ancient Egypt.

But the Greeks did not invent mathematics. That honor goes to the Egyptians. As early as 3000 BC, the Egyptians had settled into the fertile region of the upper Nile. There, they developed a society in which mathematical calculations were necessary for keeping business records, for recording taxes, and for the fair exchange of things such as food, tools, and land. The use of numbers was a logical way to keep track of daily transactions, and before long, addition and sub-traction, as well as primitive forms of multiplication and division, were used in everyday life.

Two famous documents, the Rhind and Moscow papyri, survive from around 1650 BC and show evidence of mathematical problems and equations being done. Modern-day historians have learned almost everything they know about Egyptian mathematics from these scrolls.

If the Egyptians invented mathematics, the Greeks revolutionized it. While ancient Egyptians used numbers in strictly practical ways, the Greeks used more abstract thinking to develop mathematical ideas. The Greeks moved from performing calculations for specific and practical problems to defining formulas that could be used for anything. They also invented proofs to verify that their formulas were correct. A proof would begin with a mathematical statement that was

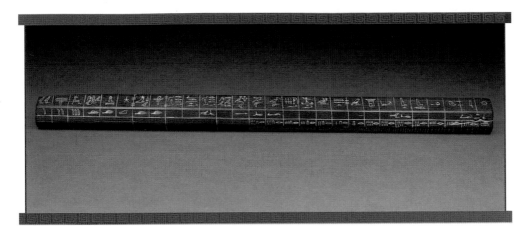

One of the first known units of measurement was the cubit. The length of a cubit varied from culture to culture, but it was generally considered to be the length from a person's elbow to the tip of their middle finger. This ancient Egyptian "cubit rod," which belonged to a scribe named Maya, is thousands of years old.

known to be true. This statement, using logic and reasoning, would be built upon to eventually ensure that a second statement was also true.

Similarly, the Greeks did not invent geometry. The Egyptians were obviously well acquainted with geometry, otherwise they never would have built pyramids to such complete perfection or understood how land could be measured and divided fairly among various owners. The Babylonians, who lived in ancient Mesopotamia (essentially the same region as present-day Iraq) in the fertile valley of the lower Euphrates and Tigris rivers between 1900 and 1600 BC, also used geometry. Archaeologists have found clay tablets in the region with numbers etched onto them, showing

that the Babylonians used math, specifically geometry, to make calculations.

But the Greeks did use geometry, and they advanced it to a form that is still used today. They used it in everyday life to divide plots of land into rectangles. The price of the plot would depend on its size. They would also use geometry in the construction of homes, courtyards, and public structures to get angles just right or to calculate how tall walls should be. Entire cities were laid out using geometric principles.

It is believed that many educated Classical Age Greeks were adept at using numbers and performing basic calculations, but very few could be considered mathematicians. The true Greek mathematicians were few and far between. It is to those few—the rarest of great thinkers—that modern mathematics truly owes its existence.

THALES

The history of Greek mathematics and mathematicians begins with Thales. Widely considered to be Europe's first philosopher, Thales was also a scientist, an astronomer, and the top geometer of his time. The exact date of Thales' birth is not known, but he is believed to have been born somewhere between 640 and 625 BC.

THALES MILESIVS.

Turpe quid aufurus, te fine tefte time.
Vita perit : mortis gloria non moritur.
Quod facturus eris, dicere diftuleris.
Crux eft, fi metuas, vincere quod nequeas.
Quum vere obiurgas, fic inimice iuvas ;
Quum falfo laudas, tunc & amice noces.
Nil nimium fatis eft. ne fit & hoc nimium.

Fac. Aufonius
Burdigalenfis, Conful.

The first known Greek philosopher, Thales of Miletus, sits before an open book in this seventeenth-century engraving. Unfortunately, all of Thales' writings are lost to time, and we know none of the specifics of his work. Some of Thales' life was recorded, however, and from these records we know that he brought geometry to Greece from Egypt.

Although Thales lived in Greece, and did well for himself as a businessman and politician in his homeland, he was restless. He yearned to travel and learn the ways of the world. With that in mind, he embarked for Egypt.

Thales learned a lot in Egypt, especially from that country's expert builders and surveyors. He saw how the surveyors measured out parcels of land for peasants. The peasants would in turn raise crops on the land and pay taxes to the Egyptian ruler—the pharaoh—as rent. Taxes were levied according to how much land each peasant worked.

Mingling with the Egyptian builders, Thales watched workers using special ropes with knots in them to measure perfect right angles. The knots were spaced at regular intervals along the rope so that the rope could be used as a measuring device. Knowing the relationship between the lengths of the three sides of a right triangle, which includes a right angle (a ninety-degree angle) between two of the sides, men could use the knotted ropes to make buildings with square walls.

Thales also learned how Egyptians used measuring sticks and the shadows those sticks cast in the sunlight to determine the height of large buildings or monuments. These calculations, too, required an understanding of triangles and the relationships between a triangle's three sides.

Thales was amazed by what he learned in Egypt. He was eager to bring his discoveries back with him to Greece and to teach what he had learned to others. Upon his return, Thales opened a school. Students flocked to him from across the Mediterranean region to learn a new subject: geometry.

The word "geometry" is from the Greek word for "land measurement." Thales also invented a unique way of teaching this subject. He used logic and reason in a systematic, step-by-step fashion, to prove the mathematical principles he used. Greek geometry, founded on the work of the builders of ancient Egypt and adapted slightly for new uses, was born.

PYTHAGORAS

One of Thales' top students was a man named Pythagoras from the Greek island of Samos. Born around 567 BC, Pythagoras learned everything he could from Thales before deciding to move on. He traveled to Egypt, where he studied geometry and astronomy. He then continued on to Babylon and many other parts of the world before returning to the Greek colony of Croton to found a new school.

Demonstration.

line *AL*, And (by the first petition) draw a right lyne from the point *A* to the point *D*, and an other from the point *C* to the point *F*. And forasmuch as the angles *B A C* and *B A G* are right angles, therfore vnto a right line *B A*, and to a point in it geuen *A*, are drawen two right lines *A C* and *A G*, not both on one and the same side, makyng the two side angles equall to two right angles: wherfore (by the 14. proposition) the lines *A C* and *A G* make directly one right line. And by the same reason the lines *B A* and *A H* make also directly one right line. And forasmuch as the angle *D B C* is equall to the angle *F B A* (for either of thē is a right angle) put the angle *A B C* common to them both: wherfore the whole angle *D B A* is equall to the

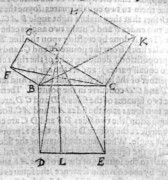

whole angle *F B C*. And forasmuch as these two lines *A B* and *B D* are equall to these two lines *B F* and *B C*, the one to the other, and the angle *D B A* is equal to the angle *F B C*: therfore (by the 4. proposition) the base *A D* is equall to the base *F C*, and the triangle *A B D* is equall to the triangle *F B C*. But (by the 41. proposition) the parallelogramme *B L* is double to the triangle *A B D*, for they haue both one and the same base, namely, *B D*, and are in the selfe same parallel lynes, that is, *B D* and *A L* and (by the same) the square *G B* is double to the triangle *F B C*, for they haue both one and the selfe same base, that is, *B F*, and are in the selfe same parallel lynes, that is, *F B* and *G C*. But the doubles of thinges equall, are (by the sixte common sentence) equall the one to the other. VVherfore the parallelograme *B L* is equall to the square *G B*. And in like sorte if (by the first petition) there be drawen a right line from the point *A* to the point *E*, and an other from the point *B* to the point *K*, we may proue ỹ the parallelograme *C L* is equal to the square *H C*. VVherfore the whole square *B D E C* is equall to the two squares *G B* and *H C*. But the square *B D E C* is described vpon the line *B C*, and the squares *G B* and *H C* are described vppon the lines *B A* & *A C*: wherfore the square of the side *B C* is equal to the squares of the sides *B A* and *A C*. VVherfore in rectangle triangles, the square whiche is made of the side that subtendeth the right angle, is equal to the squares which are made of the sides contayning the right angle: which was required to be demonstrated.

   This most excellent and notable Theoreme was first inuented of the greate philosopher Pithagoras, who for the exceeding ioy conceiued of the inuention theaof, offered in sacrifice an Oxe, as recorde Hierone, Proclus, Lycius, & Vitruuius. And it hath bene commonly called of barbarous writers of the latter time Dulcarnon.

Pithagoras the first inuenter of this proposition.

Euclid included the Pythagorean theorem in *The Elements*. Legend has it that Pythagoras went to Egypt to study on the recommendation of the philosopher Thales. At that time, Egypt was far ahead of Greece in mathematics.

The primary subject Pythagoras taught at his school was geometry. Like Thales, Pythagoras used logic to build on what he already knew was true. In this way, he could derive new theorems from ones that were already proven. He used diagrams etched into the dirt or constructed with pebbles to help him visualize his work. Only rarely did he use papyrus sheets for writing, as the material was very expensive and hard to come by.

Pythagoras's most famous contribution to geometry was the Pythagorean theorem, about which Euclid later wrote. The theorem explains the relationships between the three sides of a right triangle. Interestingly, the Pythagorean theorem was not new. The Babylonians had used this very theorem nearly 2,000 years earlier. Even the Egyptians whom Thales visited had unknowingly used the theorem when they used knotted ropes to measure right angles. Pythagoras merely devised a way to prove that the relationships between a triangle's sides are always the same. His formula was $a^2 + b^2 = c^2$. The letters "a," "b," and "c" refer to the length of each of the triangle's three sides. Side "a" multiplied by itself plus side "b" multiplied by itself equals side "c" multiplied by itself. This formula is incredibly useful in figuring out certain lengths.

Pythagoras's students were so intrigued by the man and his mathematical abilities that they formed the Pythagorean Order, an exclusive and secret group that followed Pythagoras and his teachings almost religiously. This group of people, which included members from around the known world, was said to pursue mathematical knowledge for knowledge's sake alone. They believed it was their duty to teach the things they learned.

PLATO

Sometime after Pythagoras, around 428 BC, Plato was born. Unlike Pythagoras, Plato, who lived in Athens, was primarily a philosopher, not a mathematician. He spent his days thinking about life, what it meant to exist, the differences between reality and imagination, and the differences between right and wrong. Still, he knew enough about mathematics to realize that it was an important part of any education.

Like the great thinkers who came before him, Plato, who was initially tutored by Socrates—a great philosopher known for his rational thinking and emphasis on logic—gained much of his education while traveling around the Mediterranean region. He learned everything he could about the subjects of the day. When he finally made his way back home to Athens around 387 BC, he was determined to open his own school.

Plato's school became known as the Academy, and it earned a reputation as a renowned institution for the study of philosophy, science, astronomy, music, and mathematics. For all practical purposes, Plato's contribution to mathematics ended here. The reason for this was that math was considered important at his school, but it was just one of several subjects he expected his students to master. Today, Plato's take on geometry continues to exemplify his complicated thoughts about existence and reality. Plato saw geometrical figures as ideal forms for their precision. To him, such geometrical shapes were absolutely perfect and unchanging. When such figures were found in everyday life—such as circular objects in nature, for example—he recognized that these representations of the perfect geometrical shapes were fleeting. They didn't last forever, and were far from perfect in form.

EUDOXUS

One of Plato's students at the Academy was a man by the name of Eudoxus, who lived from around

In this nineteenth-century engraving, Plato and his students gather in the garden of the Academy. Plato was one of the most influential philosophers in ancient Greece, and many of his writings survive today. Plato's school eventually came under the control of Emperor Justinian, who ordered the Academy to be closed in AD 529.

408 to 355 BC. Eudoxus, like those before him, traveled extensively as a young man, hoping to learn from people he met in distant parts of the world. He took a particular liking to astronomy, and invented mathematical formulas to explain the movements of the planets and stars.

Eudoxus eventually became well known, both as a mathematics teacher and for his theory of proportions. Euclid discussed this theory some time later in *The Elements*, a geometry textbook that for more than 2,000 years served as the definitive reference for students new to the subject. Eudoxus also developed a theory involving concentric spheres. This theory held that Earth was rooted in the center of the universe and that everything else in space, no matter how far away from Earth, revolved around it in concentric orbits. Of course, since Euclid's time, his theory of concentric spheres has been proven incorrect. Today's astronomers know that Earth is just one of many planets and other bodies in the universe that orbit the sun.

Before people understood that Earth orbited the sun, many theories were advanced to explain the motions of the stars in the sky. The concept of a geocentric (Earth-centered) system, as devised by the astronomers Ptolemy and Tycho Brahe, is illustrated in this seventeenth-century color engraving.

ARISTOTLE

Another of Plato's students, and easily his most famous, was Aristotle, who lived from 384 to 322 BC. Though Aristotle was among the youngest of the students at the Academy, he was also one of the most promising. Known as a great philosopher, Aristotle spent much of his life in deep thought, asking questions about life and existence, and proposing answers based on experience and reason.

After leaving the Academy, Aristotle went on to write and philosophize from his own school in Athens called the Lyceum. He also taught

Aristotle, depicted here in a bust from the second century BC, was an important Greek philosopher who wrote a number of books on a wide variety of subjects. The majority of Aristotle's works were lost or destroyed, but some still survive. Aristotle opened a school, known as the Lyceum, where he would lecture on philosophy.

various subjects at the Lyceum, including astronomy, physics, logic, and math. While he was not a mathematician in the strict sense of the word, he was, like many intellectuals in Classical Age Greece, interested in mathematics and how numbers helped explain the workings of the world. He saw beauty in math and knew that it was an essential component of any classical education. More important, Aristotle was a key figure in the culture of philosophical investigation into which Euclid was born. The work of Aristotle, Plato, and other great Greek thinkers helped pave the way for Euclid's great contributions to mathematics.

3 EUCLID THE MAN

Very little is known about Euclid's life. Due to a scarcity of paper, and a culture in which teaching and learning most often occurred through oral communication, relatively few historical documents exist from the days of ancient Greece. Without such documents, much of what we can conclude about Euclid amounts to little more than an educated guess.

To make matters even more difficult for historians, the name "Euclid" was very common in ancient Greece. So the texts that have been recovered must be read carefully. When "Euclid" is mentioned in writing, it's often in reference to other Euclids from the same time period. In fact, some historians have mistakenly drawn false conclusions about the most

A Man by Any Other Name

There were a lot of Euclids in Euclid's day, but perhaps the best known—other than the author of *The Elements*—was Euclid of Megara. A philosopher from the days of Plato, Euclid of Megara's legacy became forever entwined with that of the author Euclid hundreds of years after both of them were dead. It seems that translators attempting to decipher the ancient text of *The Elements* and the commentaries written about it mistook a reference to Euclid of Alexandria for a reference to Euclid of Megara. As a result, Euclid of Megara was temporarily given credit for *The Elements*, the greatest geometry book ever written.

One of ancient Greece's greatest philosophers, Plato authored *The Republic*, in which he attempted to devise the perfect government. Although Plato lived during Euclid of Megara's time, historians do not know if the two philosophers knew each other.

famous Euclid. They thought they were reading about the mathematician when, in fact, they were reading about someone else.

There was another problem. When Euclid did write, he never wrote about himself. Often authors will include at least a preface, or short introductory section, that provides background for their work and offers information about their lives. This was not so with Euclid. Euclid's surviving books contain no hints about his personal life.

For these reasons, Euclid remains somewhat of an enigma. He was a Greek mathematician who lived in the fourth and third centuries BC. His specialty was geometry, and he was known as a great teacher, perhaps the greatest of his time. He wrote *The Elements* along with a half dozen other books, and may or may not have written several more. And then, on a date that can only be guessed, and for a reason that no one will ever know, he died.

WHAT WE DO KNOW

Much of the personal information historians know about Euclid comes directly from the work of a man named Proclus. Proclus, a philosopher and

Papyrus

It may be obvious to you that the sentence you're reading now is printed on paper. But did you know that the word "paper" comes from the Egyptian word *papyrus?*

In Euclid's day books were written on papyrus. Made from the papyrus plant—a tall, woody reed found in abundance along the Nile River—papyrus took the place of stone, which, until papyrus was discovered, had been used by writers for countless centuries. Before they used papyrus, the Egyptians chipped symbols and words into rock if they hoped to leave any permanent record. Eventually, though, as written language became more and more a part of everyday life, they looked for a better and more efficient way to write. With papyrus, chipping and carving became unnecessary. Writing on papyrus was faster and easier.

To make papyrus, the first step was to chop down the reeds where they sprouted from the banks of the Nile. The reeds were then sliced into very thin strips, soaked in water until soft, and laid out on a flat surface so that the edges overlapped. The papyrus maker then took a large, heavy object, like a stone, and smashed the reeds repeatedly until they began to mesh together. The papyrus would then be left beneath a heavy object for days. This would finish the meshing process and flatten any major bumps. Finally, the new papyrus sheet would be allowed to dry.

Papyrus scrolls, which writers used whenever they had more than a few sentences to record, were made by joining individual papyrus sheets together. They could then be rolled up for storage, and unrolled for writing or reading.

Thanks to Alexander the Great's conquest of Egypt in the fourth century BC, much of the papyrus writing that survives today is in Greek. The Greeks controlled Egypt for many centuries and used papyrus to keep government records, including everything from tax documents to court proceedings. The great philosophers and teachers of the time, including Euclid, also used papyrus for their writings.

mathematician from the fifth century AD, nearly 800 years after Euclid, wrote a commentary on Euclid's most famous book, *The Elements*. Here's what he wrote, as quoted in *A History of Greek Mathematics*, translated from the Greek:

> Euclid . . . put together the *Elements*, collecting many of Eudoxus's theorems, perfecting many of Theaetetus's, and also bringing to irrefragable demonstration the

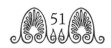

This papyrus fragment, discovered in an excavation of an archaeological site in Egypt, contains a diagram from Euclid's *The Elements*. The site, located in a town called Oxyrhynchus, has yielded many important artifacts, including a great number of ancient papyrus texts.

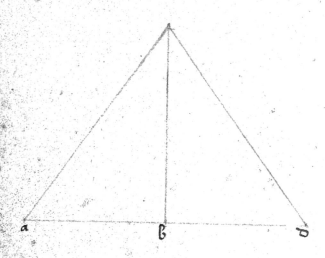

ducto   **E27.**

...o latere trianguli ī serip̄m p̄duat̄
...us quadratis que a duobus reli—
...nscribuntur:/ rectus est angulus
...orntur ¶ L.... meaz I serip̄m ducere:
...desturbeat. Est triangulus .abc.
...sub .ac./ equale quadratis duor̄ laterū
...otib̄/ duo angulus .b. on opponit̄ latuis
...zer est quedā peuarib. Apūirob .b.
...ppendiculariē sup lineā .bc. qua
...et p̄duco lineam .d c./ eus̄ p̄ pto
...um. .d c./ equale duobus quadratis .ab.
...posita est equales .ba. cōmit pp̄ gēm
...eum eynalind egualia ee quadrata
...lineam .ab. et .bd./ equalia ‖ anago
...egnale duobus quadratis .ab. et .bc.
...o pp alia rotēn staus que est ūuersa
...uos quadrata sunt egualia: est eīlez
...a c. gnare pp ortanam angulus .b.
...t rectus/ quod est propositum

...rimus liber euclidis

...liber secundus

things which were only somewhat loosely proved by his predecessors. This man lived in the time of the first Ptolemy. For Archimedes, who came immediately after the first (Ptolemy), makes mention of Euclid . . . He is then younger than the pupils of Plato, but older than Eratosthenes and Archimedes, the latter having been contemporaries, as Eratosthenes somewhere says.

Sound complicated? It is. Proclus mentions a lot of names in that passage. What he's doing, though, is using a bit of logic to determine when Euclid lived. Proclus notes that Euclid was younger than Plato's students, so he must have lived sometime after Plato. He says Euclid is older than Archimedes, so he must have lived before that famous mathematician. Finally, Proclus writes that Euclid lived in the "time of the first Ptolemy." Since we know that Ptolemy I took over Egypt after Alexander the Great's death in 323 BC, Euclid had to have been alive at that time, somewhere around 300 BC.

It's difficult to say just how accurate Proclus was in his estimations of Euclid's lifespan. Like modern-day historians, Proclus was using very old documents

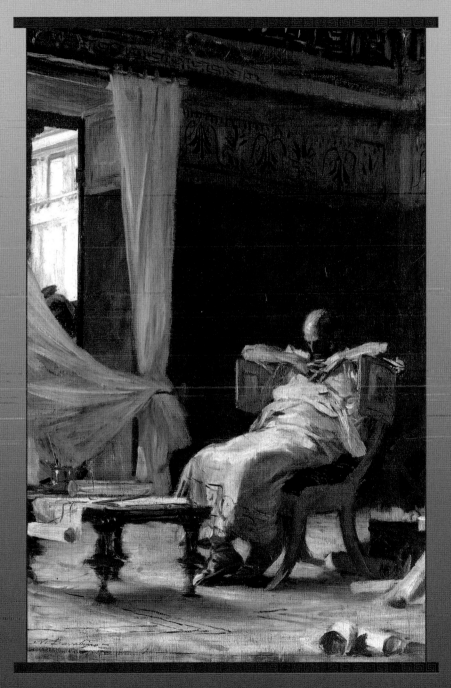

This nineteenth-century painting by Nicolò Barabino shows Archimedes deep in contemplation. Archimedes was a great mathematician and is credited with discovering the principles of density and buoyancy. Archimedes also used mathematics to design a number of machines.

and artifacts to discover clues about his subject. In this case, he had read the works of both Plato and Archimedes, as well as Euclid's *Elements*, and used all those documents to make an educated guess about Euclid's life. Just imagine doing the same now for someone who lived 800 years ago, or around 1200 AD. It wouldn't be an easy task, and it would certainly involve a lot of guesswork.

Still, Proclus's writings are all we really have to guide us through Euclid's life. Beyond that, much of

What's in a Name?

While the name Euclid was very popular during the geometer's time, that hasn't prevented some historians from speculating on its origins, or from making wild assumptions. Some authors, for instance, claim it was derived from the Arabic words *ucli* and *dis*, which mean "key" and "measurement," respectively.

Did the name "Euclid" really mean "the key to measurement"? Or even better, "the key to geometry"? Considering that Euclid was Greek, and not Arab, it's highly unlikely. But if it did mean that, you could definitely say Euclid lived up to his name.

what we have is even less of a sure thing, and therefore must be viewed with some skepticism.

THE STUDENT

Most of the great philosophers and mathematicians of ancient Greece started out as students. They studied under the respected teachers of their time, then left for a while to travel and learn from other great teachers around the world. Euclid is thought to have taken the same course. Experts today believe that anyone who wished to study mathematics in 300 BC would have to have done so in Athens, as that was the only place to find textbooks on the subject. Furthermore, in Athens there were only two schools where a mathematician of Euclid's caliber could have learned everything he did: Plato's Academy and Aristotle's Lyceum.

The Academy, remember, was the school that Plato founded around 387 BC. As Proclus concluded, Euclid was younger than the students of Plato. So we can only assume that Euclid did not have Plato himself as his teacher, but instead was educated by Plato's followers.

The Academy was a vast complex just outside of Athens. It was named in honor of the ancient Greek war hero Academos, who is said to have owned the land on which the Academy was built. Surrounded by thick stone walls, the Academy served as a public garden and was frequented by people interested in its many statues and temples to the Greek gods, or by the peace and tranquility provided by the olive trees that grew within it.

Plato's school was merely one part of the larger Academy. Based in a garden area within the Academy walls, the school became the area's top institution for the study of science and philosophy. Students who studied there had access to the Academy's athletic fields, library, a dining room where they shared meals, and the many gardens that could be found on the grounds.

Euclid would have studied all subjects taught at the Academy, not just mathematics and geometry. Astronomy, which focused on the planets and planetary movement, as well as the paths of all the stars that could be seen from the school's observatory, was one popular subject. Others included music, science, and debate.

Mathematics was Euclid's favorite subject, and he soon found himself fascinated by geometry. As Proclus said, Euclid studied the geometry of Eudoxus and

Theaetetus (c. 417–369 BC) (another philosopher and geometer), both of whom had attended the Academy before him. Euclid later included references to their work in his *Elements*. The fact that the geometry of Eudoxus and Theaetetus was included in *The Elements* is one of the reasons historians believe Euclid studied at the Academy.

Euclid is believed to have completely submerged himself in geometry at the Academy, proving himself a devoted and tireless student. Eventually, however, he found he had learned all that he could. One day, while still a young man, he packed up and moved on.

THE TEACHER

Finished with his studies at the Academy, Euclid left Athens and moved to Alexandria, Egypt. Historians are uncertain why Euclid moved to Alexandria. However, the city was a magnet for intellectuals at the time, and it only made sense for people like Euclid, who wished to learn from and converse with other great minds, to call it home.

Soon after Euclid settled into Alexandria he started his own school. Not much is known about Euclid's

Alexandria was home to this Roman theater, which could seat 800 people and dates back to the third century AD. It is believed that this theater was designed to hold musical concerts. The theater is a testament to the central role the arts played in ancient Greece, especially in Alexandria and Athens.

school, not even its name. What is known is that Euclid wrote *The Elements* shortly after he opened the school, and the primary subject taught there was mathematics.

The Elements soon gained a reputation as the best geometry text available. Anyone who hoped to master the subject had to have a copy. To get one, however, he had to transcribe the entire text by hand, line by line.

Not long after Euclid founded his school in Alexandria, Ptolemy I built the Museum, the first

national university of Egypt. Ptolemy knew that in order for the Museum to have any credibility as a great institution for learning, he had to have the best teachers. So, familiar with *The Elements*, and captivated by how clearly it demonstrated the latest developments in geometry, he decided to hire Euclid. Euclid became the Museum's very first professor of mathematics.

Likely the recipient of a respectable salary for his time, Euclid moved to the Museum and settled in with the other great teachers of the day. Along with their students, they lived, ate, researched, and shared ideas with each other. They spent long periods of time in deep thought, perhaps debating each other's theories and ideas. They spent hours in the Museum's great library, deeply absorbed in the vast collection of ancient texts stored on its shelves. The library is believed to have held more than 600,000 papyrus rolls. Scholars came to the Museum from all over the world to reference these scrolls and to use them in their studies.

Euclid quickly gained a reputation among his students and colleagues as an exceptional geometry teacher. His lectures grew increasingly popular as word spread of their quality. One day, as recounted in the writings of Proclus, Ptolemy himself sat in on one of

The Library of Alexandria was the largest library in the world at one time. It housed many rare ancient texts, all of which were lost when the library was destroyed in the late third century AD. This is an artist's reconstruction of the lost library.

Euclid's classes. He listened to what Euclid had to say. Then, according to *A History of Greek Mathematics*, wondering if perhaps there was an easier way to learn geometry, Ptolemy asked Euclid "if there was in geometry any shorter way than that of the *Elements*." Euclid replied that there was "no royal road to geometry."

Another legend, recounted by Stobaeus, a Greek philosopher writing sometime around 500 AD, tells

of one of Euclid's students asking his teacher a tough question. As recounted in *A History of Greek Mathematics*, the student asked, "What shall I get by learning these things?" Euclid called his slave and said, "Give him three pence, since he must make gain out of what he learns."

As these two stories show, Euclid must have been a good teacher, and he also must have had a good sense of humor. He challenged his students to work hard, to take the long road and not look for shortcuts. He evidently believed that anyone who hoped to master geometry had to be willing to put in the time to devote himself to the task. And if you needed money as motivation to learn, perhaps you were in the wrong field. Geometers were not wealthy.

Historians have also concluded that Euclid was probably a fair and honest man. These traits are shown in his *Elements*, in which he gives credit to both Eudoxus and Theaetetus for their indirect contributions to the book. Much of the information Euclid includes in *The Elements*, in fact, is derived from the work of those who came before him. He acknowledges this, demonstrating a respect for others and a willingness to share the intellectual spotlight. Euclid apparently knew that he would never have achieved

The Greek mathematician Eudoxus of Cnidus produced this astronomical papyrus. Eudoxus studied under Plato at the Academy and would become one of the great philosopher's most accomplished students.

Euclid's Most Famous Student: Archimedes

It is often said that a teacher's skill can be measured by the success of his or her students. If this is so, then Euclid may have been one of the best teachers ever.

Euclid, while working at the school he founded in Alexandria, is believed to have taught Archimedes, who later became known as one of the greatest Greek mathematicians. Archimedes was born around 287 BC, in the Greek colony of Syracuse. He then moved to Alexandria as a young man to attend school. Not much is known about Archimedes' school days, but many historians assume that he became fluent in the fundamentals of mathematics under the tutelage of Euclid. Euclid likely taught Archimedes everything he knew about geometry, and perhaps even encouraged him to read his books on that and other subjects.

After Archimedes finished his academic career in Alexandria, he moved back to Syracuse. There, he quickly gained a reputation as the "great geometer" and one of the most skilled mathematicians of his time. He was known for his inventions, including levers and pulleys that relied on the laws of physics to allow a single person to move exceedingly heavy objects. He made great discoveries in geometry, finding, for example, ways to derive the areas of a variety of geometric shapes.

One story recalls how Archimedes came upon what today is called Archimedes' principle. Archimedes' principle states that a body immersed wholly or partially in a fluid is buoyed up by a force equal in magnitude to the weight of the volume of fluid it displaces. Archimedes had been asked by the king whether his crown had been made of pure gold, as he was told, or a mixture of gold and some other cheaper metal, as he suspected he was being cheated.

Archimedes spent many hours searching for a way to figure out the answer to the king's question, but to no avail. And then, one day, the solution came to him as he lowered himself into his bathtub. As his body entered the tub, he noticed how the water level around him rose. His body was displacing water in proportion to his body's size. He had discovered the relationship between density and volume, a relationship that would let him determine whether the crown was pure gold. If he knew how much an object weighed, and also knew its volume, he could calculate density (density equals mass divided by volume). By comparing the density of something known to be pure gold with the calculated density of the crown, he could instantly tell if the crown was pure gold, as all pure gold must have the same density. As a result, he proved that the crown was, in fact, not pure gold and that the king was being cheated.

Archimedes died in 212 BC, during a Roman invasion of his hometown. His legend, however, lives on.

what he did without the help and contributions of those who came before him.

THE LEGEND

Amazingly, this is all we know about Euclid the man. And for that reason, it's time to move on to his writings, especially his *Elements*. In *The Elements*, we do not find clues about Euclid's life, but we do find evidence of his genius. We'll also take a look at some of Euclid's other, lesser-known works, including *Data*, *On Divisions of Figures*, *Phaeno-mena*, and *Optics*. By gaining some idea of what each of these texts did to advance science and mathe-matics, something can be learned about Euclid's mind. Euclid was an explorer, a man unafraid to step into the unknown. He took his subject, which he had mas-tered, to a new level. He did more

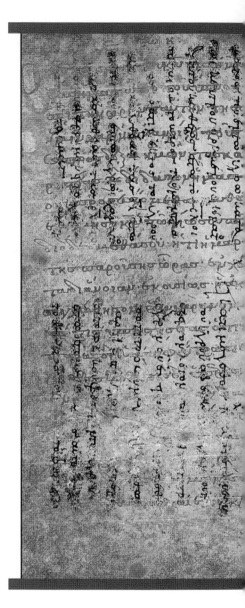

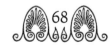

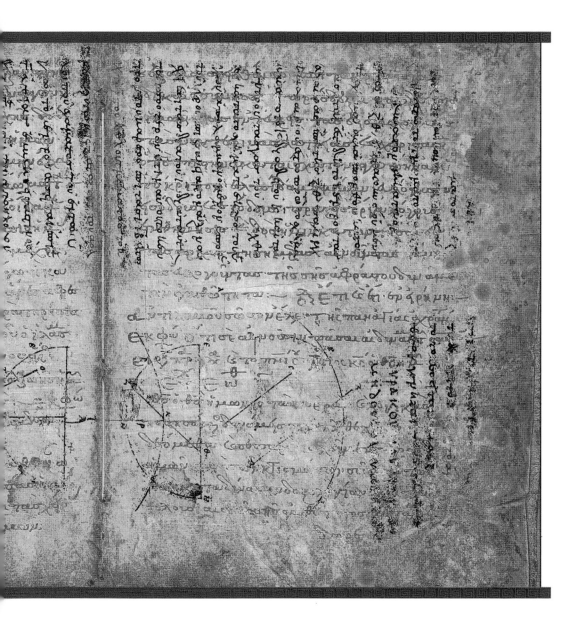

The *Archimedes Palimpsest* is a work by Archimedes that was recovered in the twentieth century. Before paper or parchment was widely available, it was common for scribes to copy over old manuscripts. In the twelfth century, a scribe took pages from a copy of one of Archimedes' manuscripts and used them for a Christian liturgical text.

for geometry and the understanding of geometry than anyone before him or, some say, anyone who followed. By writing *The Elements*, the definitive textbook on geometry, he explained the subject he loved for all who cared to learn.

4 Euclid's Work

Euclid would probably not be known were it not for his greatest and most famous work, *The Elements*. It is unclear when, exactly, Euclid wrote *The Elements*. In fact, the original copy of the book is lost.

What is clear, though, is that the book, written on nothing more than a papyrus scroll, changed the subject of geometry forever. *The Elements*, widely considered a work of genius unlike any mathematical text that came before it, took a vast and disorganized array of geometric progress accumulated over hundreds of years and brought it all together into one clear and concise work. It made geometry much easier to understand. More important, it introduced an entirely new way of presenting complicated information through its unique structure.

The first English edition of *The Elements* was published in 1570 by a man named John Dee. Dee's primary interest outside of science was magic and the supernatural. He was considered to be one of the most brilliant minds of his age.

Because the original copy of *The Elements* is missing, it's impossible to know for sure what was in the original text. The copies we have today are translated versions of other copies made hundreds of years ago. Euclid's students couldn't run out to the bookstore and purchase an official copy of *The Elements* for class. If they wanted the book, they probably had to sit down and copy the original by hand. This would have been very tedious work. Some students may have cut corners, perhaps just taking down the information they thought they needed. It's no surprise, then, that most experts believe *The Elements* of today is likely very different from the one Euclid wrote more than 2,000 years ago.

THE GREAT IDEA

Euclid's idea to take everything that was known about geometry and organize it to make it clear and easy to follow was not new. In fact, other geometers had already tried it. But the task was huge, and Euclid succeeded where the others failed.

What did Euclid do different from those who came before him? He started from scratch. He took the most

basic ideas—the same ideas others had often ignored—and then built upon them. He approached geometry as a carpenter might approach building a house. He began with the foundation, made sure it was solid, then built in stages from there. When he was through, his "house," his *Elements*, stood strong.

THE BOOKS OF *THE ELEMENTS*

Euclid wrote *The Elements* in thirteen separate books. Each book tackled a different aspect of geometry, but each was laid out in similar fashion. To understand how *The Elements* was organized, let's take a look at book I, which is about "plane geometry." Plane geometry deals with plane figures, that is, objects with flat surfaces.

Book I begins with a series of simple definitions. Some of these definitions (as they appear in *The Thirteen Books of Euclid's Elements*, by Euclid) you may have heard of, especially if you've had any exposure to geometry:

1. A point is that which has no part.

2. A line is breadthless length.

3. The extremities of a line are points.

4. A straight line is a line which lies evenly with points on itself.

5. A surface is that which has length and breadth only.

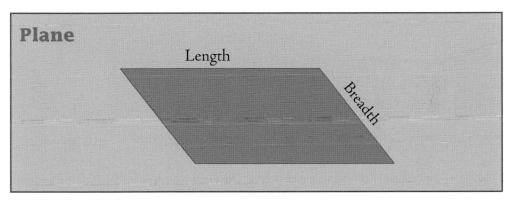

There are a total of twenty-three definitions in the first book. Here are a few more:

11. An obtuse angle is an angle greater than a right angle.

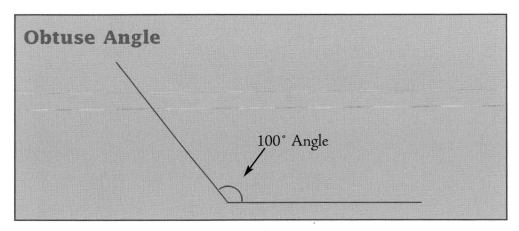

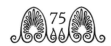

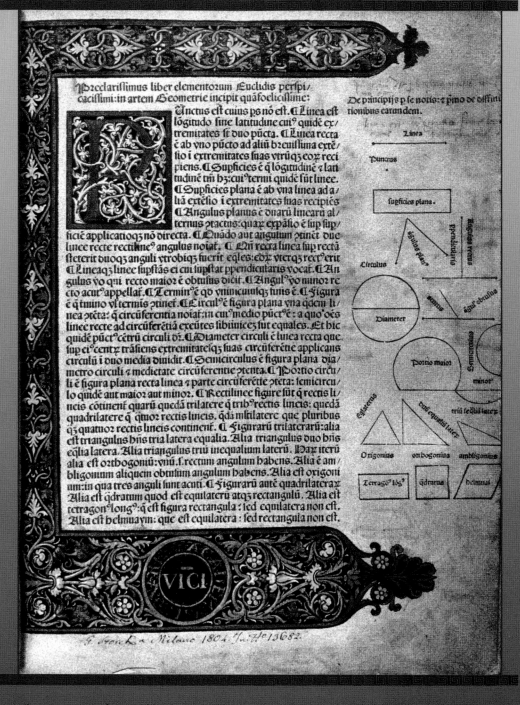

This page is from the first published edition of *The Elements*, which was printed in 1482. *The Elements* has been printed more times than any book besides the Bible.

15. A circle is a plane figure contained by one line such that all the straight lines falling upon it from one point among those lying within the figure are equal to one another.

16. And the point is called the center of the circle.

The last definition in the book deals with what is meant by "parallel."

23. Parallel straight lines are straight lines which, being in the same plane and being produced indefinitely in both directions, do not meet one another in either direction.

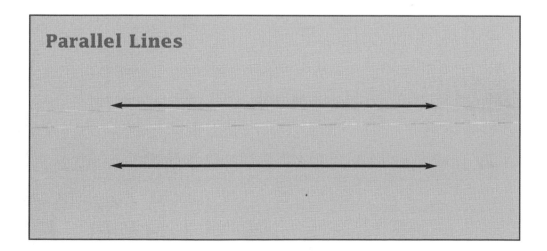

Parallel Lines

Following the definitions, book I lists five "postulates." The postulates use the same words Euclid defined in his twenty-three definitions. That way there's no question as to what is meant. If the reader is confused, all he or she has to do is refer back to the definitions for guidance. The first three postulates covered the ways in which a person can construct a geometric figure. As Euclid wrote, one can do so:

1. by drawing a straight line from any point to any point

2. by producing a finite straight line continuously in a straight line

3. by describing a circle with any center and distance

The last two postulates in book I are as follows:

4. All right angles are equal to one another.

5. If a straight line falling on two straight lines make the interior angles on the same side less than two right angles, the two straight lines, if produced indefinitely,

meet on that side on which are the angles less than the two right angles.

Euclid followed up his postulates with a list of "common notions." The common notions are what today we would call axioms. An axiom is a self-evident truth. It's obviously true to anyone who reads it.

Euclid includes five common notions in book I. All five are about equality.

1. Things which are equal to the same thing are also equal to one another.

2. If equals be added to equals, the wholes are equal.

3. If equals be subtracted from equals, the remainders are equal.

4. Things which coincide with one another are equal to one another.

5. The whole is greater than the part.

You might notice something about Euclid's style. He's very orderly. Everything comes in a neat package,

clearly presented for easy reading. He uses logic. He doesn't jump from one idea to another completely unrelated idea. Instead, he uses each idea to build, logically, to the next one.

The rest of *The Elements* is full of more definitions, problems, diagrams, and enough challenging geometry to keep any student of the subject busy for years. Book II, for example, delves into the geometry of rectangles. Book III is about circles. Book XII covers areas and volumes.

Historians of mathematics will never know for sure which parts of *The Elements* came entirely from Euclid and which relied in whole or in part on the work of earlier geometers and mathematicians. All agree, however, that that's not the point. The genius of *The Elements*, they'll tell you, is not in where the information came from. It's how that information is presented, and how that presentation changed geometry forever.

DATA, *ON DIVISIONS OF FIGURES*, PHAENOMENA, AND *OPTICS*

While *The Elements* was, by far, Euclid's most famous and respected work, it was by no means all he had to offer the world. In fact, for his time, Euclid was quite

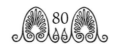

The Fifth Postulate

Euclid's most famous postulate is his fifth. It's the postulate he later uses as the foundation for a discussion on parallel lines. Here it is again: "If a straight line falling on two straight lines make the interior angles on the same side less than two right angles, the two straight lines, if produced indefinitely, meet on that side on which are the angles less than the two right angles."

Why is this postulate so well known? For one, it's long and complicated—far more so than any of the others. But that's not what attracts mathematicians. Ever since Euclid wrote it, math experts have called it inadequate because there is no way to prove it is true. Euclid himself had questions about the fifth postulate. He tried to find a way to prove its truth, but could not. In the end, he decided it was impossible to do so.

This, of course, presented Euclid with a problem. Since he couldn't prove the postulate true, how would he continue on with his book, in which everything written depended on everything before it? If his foundation wasn't solid, how would he build? Euclid's solution was simple. He just assumed the fifth postulate was true, and he moved on.

While this may have satisfied Euclid, it didn't make the skeptics happy. For hundreds of years, mathematicians around the world did everything they could to prove the fifth postulate, but no one succeeded.

Some geometers instead offered provable alternatives to the fifth postulate that they believed could be used in its place. One of the most famous of these alternatives was what is today called Playfair's axiom after John Playfair, a Scottish mathematician who lived in the late eighteenth and early nineteenth centuries. "Through a given point in a plane, one and only one line can be drawn parallel to a given line." Playfair's axiom is well known today among beginning geometry students because it's relatively easy to understand. Of course, just because something is easy doesn't mean it's any better, and most experts agreed that Playfair's was not good enough to replace the fifth postulate. So, the fifth postulate remained, forever a part of Euclid's *Elements*.

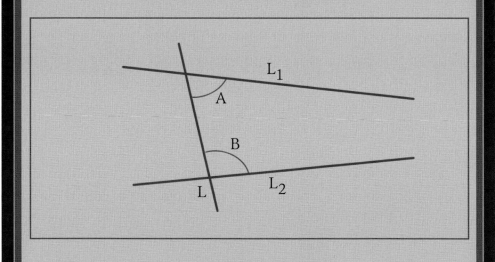

a productive author. He is believed to have written many different books, some of which have survived through the ages, and others of which have apparently disappeared forever. All of the books we have today that are attributed to Euclid are on mathematics. All have been essentially ignored because of their relative lack of importance when compared to *The Elements*. For us, however, these books play an important role in helping us understand just who Euclid was. Unlike *The Elements*, which for the most part compiled and organized the material of Euclid's predecessors, these other books—including *Data*, *On Divisions of Figures*, *Phaenomena*, and *Optics*—cover his personal work in mathematics.

Data discusses geometrical proofs in plane geometry. In a proof—an essential part of geometry and all mathematics—the mathematician uses logic and reason to establish the truth of a statement. *On Divisions of Figures* covers the division of geometric figures into smaller parts. *Phaenomena* delves into how geometry can be used in astronomy. *Optics* deals with the geometry of vision and perspectives. For example, how, from very far away, something that is big can look small to the human eye.

These books all show that Euclid was, first and foremost, a mathematician. He must have been fascinated

neq; mutuò cocurrét, neque erut paralleli.

Sit rurſus planū ſpeculum α γ, oculus autē 6, radii verò reflexi 6
γ δ, 6 α ε. dico duos hos radios reflexos γ δ,
& α ε, neque parallelos eſſe, neque produ-
ctos ad partes δ & ε, poſſe concurrere: quia
enim æqualis eſt angulus ζ, angulo θ, & angulus κ angulo μ, maior autem eſt angulus ζ angulo κ, propterea quòd eſt extrin-
ſecùs angulus, in triangulo 6 α γ. maior
igitur eſt angulus ζ angulo μ. Quare radii
reflexi γ δ & α ε, neque paralleli inter ſe
ſunt, neque concurrent ad partes ε & δ.

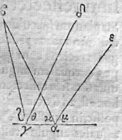

IN CONVEXO SPECVLO.

Sit rurſus conuexùm ſpeculum α κ ζ γ, o-
cuius autem 6, radii autem reflexi 6 ζ δ, 6 κ
ε. dico radios reflexos ζ δ & κ ε, neque parallelos eſſe, nec poſſe cocurrere ad partes
ε, δ. Connectatur enim recta κ ζ, & produ-
catur vtrinque ad ο & κ · Quia igitur angulus 6 ζ γ æqualis eſt angulo δ ζ λ, eò ꝗ
radii ad æquales angulos reflectuntur, maior igitur eſt angulus δ ζ μ, angulo 6 ζ κ.
& angulus 6 ζ κ, maior angulo 6 κ μ, &

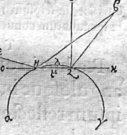

angulus 6 κ μ. maior eſt angulo ε κ α. angulus enī 6 κ λ, æqualis eſt
angulo ε κ α maior igitur eſt δ ζ μ angulus, angulo ε κ α. multò
igitur maior eſt angulus δ ζ μ, angulo ε κ ο. igitur radii ζ δ, κ ε, neque concurrent, neque paralleli erunt.

THEOREMA 5.

In cauis ſpeculis ſi oculum colloces aut in centro, aut in circunferentia, aut extra circúferétiã, id eſt, inter cétrū & circúferé-tiã, radii reflexi cócurrét.

Sit cauum ſpeculum α γ δ, centrum autem ſphæræ, cuius portio eſt ipſum ſpeculum concauum, ſit 6, in quo ponatur
oculus, ab eóque ad circunferentiã du-
cantur radii 6 α 6 γ, 6 δ· æquales igitur
ſunt anguli poſiti ad puncta α, γ, δ· ſunt

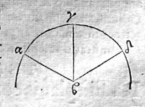

enim

enim anguli femicirculorum. Radii igitur 6 α, 6 γ, 6 δ, ab oculo ad
fpeculum misfi, in fe ipfos reflectétur: id enim oftenfum eft. Quare concurrent in puncto 6.

OCVLVS IN CIRCVNFERENTIA.

Sit cauum fpeculum α γ θ 6, oculus autem
fit 6, collocetúrque in ipfius fpeculi circú-
ferentia, & ab oculo 6 profiliant radii 6 γ,
6 α, qui reflectantur ad puncta δ, ε. Quia
segmentum α γ 6, maius eft fegmento 6 θ
γ·maior igitur eft 6 α γ angulus, angulo 6
γ θ. Quare angulus ε α κ (per primam pro-
pofitionem) maior eft angulo δ γ α. duo
igitur anguli 6 α γ, ε α κ, maiores funt duobus angulis 6 γ θ, & δ γ α. quare reliquus
angulus 6 α ε, reliquo angulo δ γ 6, minor eft, ac multò etiá minor ipfo δ ν 6. igitur radii reflexi γ δ, α ε, concurrent ad eas partes, in quibus eft ζ·idem oftendetur oculo pofito extra circunfe-
rentian, vt in fequenti theoremate.

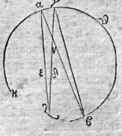

THEOREMA 6.

In cauis fpeculis, fi inter centrum & circunferentiam colloces oculum, radii reflexi interdum concurrent, interdum non
concurrent.

Sit cauum fpeculú α γ, cuius centrú δ, oculus autē ponatur in pú-
cto 6, inter centrum & circunferentiam: radii verò fint 6 α, 6 γ,
qui reflectantur ad puncta κ & ζ, ipfi autē
radii ad fpeculum vfque protrahátur, qui
fint α θ, γ κ. Iam radius α θ aut maior eft,
aut minor, aut æqualis radio γ κ. Si ergo
radius α θ, æqualis fit radio γ κ, æqualis e-
tiam eft circunferentia α γ θ, circunferé-
tiæ γ α κ. Quare angulus μ æqualis erit á-
gulo ξ · æqualium enim fectionum anguli
funt inter fe æquales. duo item anguli μ &
λ, æquales erunt duobus angulis ν & ξ. pp-
ter æqualitatem angulorum reflexionis & incidentiæ. Quocirca
reliquus angulus o, æqualis erit reliquo angulo π. igitur ϱ angulus
maior erit angulo o. quia enim angulus ϱ, maior eft angulo π (eft

H   enim

by shapes, numbers, and ratios, and must have wondered how they applied to everyday life. As one of the leading thinkers in a time of great progress and excitement, Euclid must have spent countless hours pondering the significance of his work. Perhaps he realized that one day his thoughts on mathematics would lead to something big.

OTHER TEXTS

Some historians believe Euclid wrote still other books that have since disappeared. To back up their claims, they cite the writings of other ancient philosophers and mathematicians who sometimes refer to a Euclid in their works and give Euclid credit for certain texts. But these texts are lost forever, so it's impossible to know for sure if Euclid truly did have a part in their creations.

One book, called *Catoptrica*, is still in print today, although it's likely very different from the original version. It discusses reflection and uses geometry to explain it. While some experts doubt Euclid had anything to do with this book, others believe at least a portion of its material is derived from his work.

Other books that some believe are Euclid's cannot be found anywhere. In *Pseudaria*—a book that Proclus,

the early philosopher, called "The Book of Fallacies"— Euclid supposedly demonstrated how many of the ideas about geometry during and prior to his time were wrong. He apparently did so through the use of his proven theorems, which time and time again showed that the old conclusions had to be in error.

Another text that is attributed to Euclid but is nowhere to be found is *Surface-Loci*. Supposedly written as two separate books, *Surface-Loci* is said to have discussed the geometric relationships between points found on surfaces.

Still another book, *Porisms*, is believed to have delved deeply into complicated geometry. Some experts think this book would have shown Euclid to have been a far more advanced mathematician than he is given credit for being.

Three other books that some attribute to Euclid, but which most disregard completely when discussing his work, are *The Elements of Music*, *Sectio Canonis*, and *Introduction to Harmony*. All three are about sound. In addition, some have said Euclid may have authored several texts about mechanics, the science and physics behind movement. In all these cases there is no conclusive evidence to prove that Euclid is the author. Although each book may contain details that are suspiciously similar to Euclid's known works, none are definitely his. This very fact—that so many books without known authors are commonly attributed to Euclid—attests to Euclid's lasting influence. Even in death, thousands of years after he thought and wrote and lived, his ideas survive in the works of others.

Euclid, a product of the life and times that surrounded him in 300 BC, had an incredible intellectual vision. He turned to the works of his predecessors to launch his own career pursuing a subject that both fascinated and challenged him. During his life, Euclid was well respected by his peers. For the most part, his fellow citizens—including Greek philosophers, mathematicians, and scientists—looked up to him. They saw him as an innovator, as a man who was unafraid to take big new steps in his field and risk the criticisms of those who might disagree. He was everything one might expect in an intellectual leader of ancient Greece.

Those who did find fault in Euclid's work were probably unhappy with his unwavering attention to every last detail. They questioned why this man saw it

This page of geometrical figures is from a twelfth-century copy of one of Euclid's works. Only four of Euclid's works, not counting *The Elements*, have survived. Many of Euclid's works were translated into other languages and studied by mathematicians throughout the world.

necessary to include the simplest of mathematical proofs to prove something that to them seemed completely obvious. Perhaps they believed there were more important things to do than break geometry down to its elements, as Euclid had done. They didn't see the genius in Euclid's move toward the basics.

Upon Euclid's death, not much changed. Or at least not right away. He still had both critics and enthusiasts. Eventually, though, his fame and reputation grew as *The Elements* became known as the best book available for beginning mathematics students. *The Elements* was required reading for any aspiring mathematician. In a region where education and learning were valued in the same way as the democratic freedoms of speech and debate, Euclid's book was critically important. It was a symbol of progress, and perhaps of a future where mathematics would play an even greater role in the workings of the world.

Over time, as might be expected, people forgot about Euclid the person. But even as his life faded from memory, his greatest work lived on. Many commentaries were written on *The Elements*. Designed to help guide students in their reading, these commentaries, most of which are now lost, sometimes found mistakes in Euclid's work, but more often than not

Adaptations

It is believed that prior to the 1800s, most copies of *The Elements* in circulation around the world were in fact based not on Euclid's original text, but on an adaptation of it by another ancient Greek. Sometime in the late 300s, more than 600 years after Euclid's death, a mathematician named Theon of Alexandria decided he would edit the book to make it easier to read and to fix some errors he had found. He made many changes to the original and even incorporated the works of other authors into the text.

When he was finished, his version of *The Elements* was, in many ways, quite different from Euclid's. Unfortunately, those who lived after Theon used his copy of *The Elements*, and not Euclid's (which by then would have been extremely hard to find) to produce further editions. It wasn't until 1818 that an edition was produced that is believed to be much closer to Euclid's original.

wound up praising the author for his immeasurable contributions to mathematics.

Over hundreds of years, handwritten copies of *The Elements* were distributed around the world. These copies came in many different translations and were read by thousands of eager young students. The first printed edition of *The Elements* was produced in 1482, nearly 1,800 years after Euclid wrote the book and just ten years before Christopher Columbus sailed to the Americas from Spain. It took almost another century for the first English edition of the book to appear in 1570. Since then, many more editions have been printed. Some of these editions have been edited and shortened, tailored to modern-day readers. Other editions have attempted to remain as close as possible to the original manuscript as written by Euclid.

Today, Euclid's legacy continues, as high school geometry students are regularly taught the basics of the subject through passages from *The Elements*. Geometry textbooks often quote Euclid's work and commonly use his examples and proofs to illustrate important points. Indeed, were it not for Euclid, proofs themselves may have never become the standard in mathematics as they are today.

Geometry, and mathematics in general, has changed a lot since Euclid's day, but much also remains the same. People today turn to *The Elements* to learn about the foundations of mathematics—to see where it all began and to learn the subject from the ground up. After all, there's no point in trying to understand Einstein's theory of relativity, or any of the other highly advanced mathematical concepts of today, if you don't

The discoveries Euclid made in the field of geometry are still being taught today. These eighth-grade students learn about the properties of Platonic solids, which Euclid wrote about in *The Elements*. The fact that *The Elements* is still being read today is a testament to its stature as one of the greatest mathematical works ever produced.

have a solid grasp of the fundamentals. In 1783, the great German philosopher Immanuel Kant wrote, "There is no book at all in metaphysics such as we have in mathematics. If you want to know what mathematics is, just look at Euclid's *Elements*," according to *Euclid: The Creation of Mathematics.*

Immanuel Kant, seen here in an eighteenth-century portrait, was a German philosopher who wrote about *The Elements*. Kant is considered to be one of Germany's greatest philosophers. He produced a number of books during his lifetime and was influenced by Euclid's works.

Just one of the many mathematicians who owe a great debt to Euclid, Isaac Newton is credited with outlining the laws of gravity, the laws of motion, and developing the ideas that would serve as the foundation for modern calculus. This 1847 painting by Hermann Goldschmidt shows Newton as a young man.

Euclid's life may be a mystery, but his legacy is well known. The great mathematicians who followed Euclid—from Archimedes to Galileo to Sir Isaac Newton—all studied his work. And all, not surprisingly, were profoundly influenced by it, as traces of Euclid's ideas and methods are evident in their own contributions to math and science. The fact is, the world as we know it now—even though it's very different than it was 2,000 years ago—wouldn't be the same without Euclid. This man, the founding father of geometry, could not have known what his book would do for those who followed him. But if he had, he certainly would have been pleased.

TIMELINE

circa 800 BC	The first Olympic Games are held, marking the beginning of the ancient Greek period.
circa 640 BC	Thales is born.
circa 600 BC	The dawn of Greek democracy.
circa 567 BC	Pythagoras is born.
circa 470 BC	Socrates is born.
circa 428 BC	Plato is born.
384 BC	Aristotle is born.
circa 356 BC	Alexander the Great is born.
336 BC	Philip II is assassinated, and his son, Alexander, becomes king of Macedon.
circa 325 BC	Euclid is born.

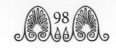

323 BC	Alexander the Great dies, marking the end of the ancient Greek period and the beginning of the Hellenistic Age.
circa 300 BC	Euclid completes *The Elements*.
circa 287 BC	Archimedes is born.
circa 265 BC	Euclid dies.
146 BC	Greece is integrated into the Roman Empire, marking the end of the Hellenistic Age.
circa AD 410	Proclus is born.
AD 1482	First printed edition of *The Elements* appears.
AD 1570	First English edition of *The Elements* appears.

GLOSSARY

Classical Age A period (490–323 BC) in ancient Greece characterized by progress in art, architecture, science, democracy, and other ideals of the time.

commentary A written interpretation, explanation, or critique of someone else's work.

democracy A system of government in which people are granted a voice in civic and political affairs.

geometry A branch of mathematics that deals with the measurement, properties, and relationships of points, lines, angles, surfaces, and solids.

mathematics The science of numbers and their relationships.

papyrus A type of paper made from a tall, woody reed plant.

parallel Two lines that extend in the same direction but do not meet.

philosopher One who seeks wisdom.

postulate A claim that is put forth and accepted as true.

predecessor One who comes before.

proof A method used in mathematics to establish the truth of a mathematical statement.

scroll A roll of material on which documents may be written.

skeptic A person who doubts whether something is true.

theorem A statement in mathematics shown to be true through the logical use of other previously established truths.

For More Information

American Mathematical Society
201 Charles Street
Providence, RI 02904-2294
(800) 321-4AMS (4267)
e-mail: ams@ams.org
Web site: http://www.ams.org

American Museum of Natural History
Central Park West at 79th Street
New York, NY 10024-5192
(800) 462-8687
Web site: http://www.amnh.org

The Ancient Philosophy Society
4554 Mayflower Hill
Colby College
Waterville, ME 04901
(207) 872-3140
e-mail: jpgordon @colby.edu
Web site: http://www.trincoll.edu/orgs/aps

The British Museum
Great Russell Street
London, England WC1B 3DG
(+44) 020 7323 8299
e-mail: information@thebritishmuseum.ac.uk
Web site: http://www.thebritishmuseum.ac.uk

Carnegie Museum of Natural History
4400 Forbes Avenue
Pittsburgh, PA 15213
(412) 622-3131
e-mail: cmnhweb@CarnegieMNH.org
Web site: http://www.CarnegieMNH.org

The Center for Hellenic Studies
3100 Whitehaven Street NW
Washington, DC 20008
(202) 745-4400
Web site: http://www.chs.harvard.edu

Institute for Byzantine and
Modern Greek Studies, Inc.
115 Gilbert Road
Belmont, MA 02178-2200
(617) 484-6595
Web site: http://www.orthodoxinfo.com/ibmgs

Northwest Center for Philosophy for Children
P.O. Box 353350
Department of Philosophy
University of Washington
Seattle, WA 98195
e-mail: info@philosophyforchildren.org
Web site: http://depts.washington.edu/nwcenter

WEB SITES

Due to the changing nature of Internet links, the Rosen Publishing Group, Inc. has developed an online list of Web sites related to the subject of this book. This site is updated regularly. Please use this link to access the list:

http://www.rosenlinks.com/lgp/eucl

FOR FURTHER READING

Artmann. Benno. *Euclid: The Creation of Mathematics.* New York, NY: Springer-Verlag New York, Inc., 1999.

Asimov, Isaac. *Great Ideas of Science.* Boston, MA: Houghton Mifflin, 1969.

Courant, Richard, and Herbert Robbins, revised by Ian Stewart. *What Is Mathematics?: An Elementary Approach to Ideas and Methods.* New York, NY: Oxford University Press, 1996.

Cuomo, S. *Ancient Mathematics.* London, England: Routledge, 2001.

Heath, Sir Thomas. *History of Greek Mathematics.* New York, NY: Dover Publications, Inc., 1981.

Heath, Sir Thomas. *A Manual of Greek Mathematics.* New York, NY: Dover Publications, Inc., 2003.

Hull, Robert E. *Everyday Life: World of Ancient Greece.* Danbury, CT: Grolier Publishing, 1999.

Kahn, Charles H. *Pythagoras and the Pythagoreans: A Brief History.* Indianapolis, IN: Hackett Publishing Company, Inc., 2001.

McGinnis, Maura. *Greece: A Primary Source Cultural Guide.* New York, NY: Rosen Publishing Group, 2004.

Muir, Jane. *Of Men & Numbers: The Story of the Great Mathematicians*. New York, NY: Dover Publications, Inc., 1996.

Nardo, Don. *Philosophy and Science in Ancient Greece: The Pursuit of Knowledge* (Lucent Library of Historical Eras). Farmington Hills, MI: Lucent Books, 2004.

Pearson, Anne. *Eyewitness: Ancient Greece*. New York, NY: DK Publishing, 2000.

Reimer, Luetta, and Wilbert Reimer. *Mathematicians Are People, Too: Stories from the Lives of Great Mathematicians*. Palo Alto, CA: Dale Seymour Publications, 1990.

Williams, Susan. *The Greeks*. New York, NY: Thomson Learning, 1993.

BIBLIOGRAPHY

Artmann, Benno. *Euclid: The Creation of Mathematics*. New York, NY: Springer-Verlag New York, Inc., 1999.

Berggren, J. L., and R. S. D. Thomas. *Euclid's Phaenomena: A Translation and Study of a Hellenistic Treatise in Spherical Astronomy*. New York, NY: Garland Publishing Inc., 1996.

Boyer, Carl B. *A History of Mathematics*. New York, NY: John Wiley & Sons, Inc., 1968.

Craig, Edward, ed. "Geometry, Philosophical Issues In." In *Routledge Encyclopedia of Philosophy*, Vol. 4. London, England: Routledge, 1998.

Cuomo, S. *Ancient Mathematics*. London, England: Routledge, 2001.

Euclid. *The Thirteen Books of Euclid's Elements*. New York, NY: Dover Publications, Inc., 1956.

Heath, Sir Thomas. *A History of Greek Mathematics*, Vol. 1, *From Thales to Euclid*. New York, NY: Dover Publications, Inc., 1981.

Hellenic Ministry of Culture. "Plato's Academy." Retrieved December 29, 2004 (http://www.culture.gr/2/21/211/21103a/e211ca03.html).

Hornblower, Simon, and Antony Spawforth, eds. *The Oxford Companion to Classical Civilization*. New York, NY: Oxford University Press, 1998.

The Internet Encyclopedia of Philosophy. "The Academy." Retrieved December 29, 2004 (http://www.iep.utm.edu/a/academy.htm).

Speake, Graham, ed. "Euclid." In *Encyclopedia of Greece and the Hellenic Tradition*, Vol. 1. London, England: Fitzroy Dearborn Publishers, 2000.

Terry, Leon. *The Mathmen*. New York, NY: McGraw-Hill Book Company, 1964.

Young, Robyn V., ed. "Euclid of Alexandria." In *Notable Mathematicians: From Ancient Times to the Present*. Detroit, MI: Gale Research, 1998.

INDEX

A

Academos, 58
Academy, the, 41, 45, 57–59
Alexander the Great, 14,
    21–25, 51
 death of, 25–26, 54
Alexandria, 26, 59, 60, 66
Archimedes, 54, 56,
    66–67, 97
Archimedes' principle, 67
Aristotle, 25, 45–46, 57
Athens, 14–20, 26, 40, 45,
    57, 59
 and citizenship, 17–20
 Public Assembly, 20

B

Babylon/Babylonians, 33–34,
    37, 39

C

Catoptrica, 86
Classical Age, 11, 14, 25, 29,
    34, 46

D

Data, 68, 83

democratic/democracy,
    13–14, 16, 20, 21
 Athenian versus modern,
    17, 20
 Demokratia, 14
Diadochi, 25–26
Divisions of Figures, On,
    68, 83

E

Earth, 43–44
Elements, The, 43, 48, 49,
    51, 56, 59, 60, 61, 62,
    63, 68, 70, 71, 83, 91,
    93, 94
 adaptations of, 92
 fifth postulate, 78, 81–82
 identity of author, 48
 mistakes in, 91, 92
 preservation/copying of,
    60, 73, 92
 summary of, 74–80
 uniqueness of, 73–74,
    79–80
Elements of Music, The, 87
Eratosthenes, 54
Euclid
 education of, 57, 58–59
 lifespan of, 54

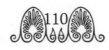

ABOUT THE AUTHOR

Chris Hayhurst is a writer living in New York. His interest in both philosophy and mathematics can be traced to high school, where he first read Plato and discovered pi, and to college, where he was exposed to the teachings of Socrates and other great philosophers.

PHOTO CREDITS

Cover, pp. 3, 45 Erich Lessing/Art Resource, NY; Cover (inset), p. 3 (inset) © Alinari Archives/Corbis; p. 8 British Museum, London/Bridgeman Art Library; pp. 10, 18 Scala/Art Resource, NY; pp. 14–15 akg-images; p. 21 Ancient Art and Architecture Collection Ltd./Bridgeman Art Library; p. 22 The Art Archive/ Archaeological Museum Naples/Dagli Orti; pp. 22–23 Originally published in Historical Atlas of the World, © J. W. Cappelens Forlag A/S, Oslo, 1962. Maps by Berit Lie. Used with permission of J. W. Cappelens Forlag; p. 24, 55 Alinari/Art Resource, NY; p. 27 The Art Archive/Jan Vinchon Numismatist Paris/Dagli Orti; pp. 30–31 © The British Museum/HIP/Art Resource, NY; p. 33 Réunion des Musées Nationaux/Art Resource, NY; p. 35 Biblio- thèque Nationale, Paris, France, Giraudon/Bridgeman Art Library; pp. 38, 72, 76, 84–85 © History of Science Collections, University of Oklahoma Libraries; pp. 42–43, 90 Bibliothèque Nationale, Paris, France/Archives Charmet/Bridgeman Art Library; p. 44 Stapleton Collection, UK/Bridgeman Art Library; p. 48 Bildarchiv Preussischer Kulturbesitz/Art Resource, NY; p. 52–53 University of Pennsylvania; p. 60 akg-images/Werner Forman; p. 62 Stefan Viljoen; p. 64–65 Réunion des Musées Nationaux/Art Resource, NY; pp. 68–69 © Christie's Images Ltd; pp. 75, 77, 82 by Tahara Anderson; p. 94 Hulton Archive/Getty Images; p. 95 Private Collection/Bridgeman Art Library; p. 96 Academie des Sciences, Paris, France/Archives Charmet/Bridgeman Art Library.

Designer: Tahara Anderson
Editor: Nicholas Croce
Photo Researcher: Jeffrey Wendt